Step into Winter
A New Season

by Jane Belk Moncure
illustrated by Linda Hohag
color by Lori Jacobson

Created by

Distributed by CHILDRENS PRESS®
Chicago, Illinois

Grateful appreciation is expressed to Elizabeth Hammerman, Ed. D., Science Education Specialist, for her services as consultant.

CHILDRENS PRESS HARDCOVER EDITION
ISBN 0-516-08127-6

CHILDRENS PRESS PAPERBACK EDITION
ISBN 0-516-48127-4

Library of Congress Cataloging in Publication Data

Moncure, Jane Belk.
    Step into winter : a new season / by Jane Belk Moncure ; illustrated by Linda Hohag ; color by Lori Jacobson ; created by Child's World.
        p. cm. — (Discovery world)
    Summary: Describes the various aspects of winter in brief text and illustrations.
    ISBN 0-89565-574-8
    1. Winter—Juvenile literature.   2. Natural history—Juvenile literature.   [1. Winter.]   I. Hohag, Linda, ill.   II. Child's World (Firm)   III. Title.   IV. Series.
QH81.M745   1990
574.5'43—dc20   90-30636
                                                                                CIP
                                                                                AC

1 2 3 4 5 6 7 8 9 10 11 12 R 99 98 97 96 95 94 93 92 91 90

Step into Winter
A New Season

Winter is here. How can you tell? Pull on
your snow boots and grab your cap.

Let's take a walk through the coldest
season of the year. Here we go!

You can tell winter is here because the wind is icy cold. Snowflakes are whirling and twirling all around. Catch some in your hands.

Look closely. How many different snowflakes can you find before the tiny crystals of ice melt away?

Shake the snow off a tree branch. All the leaves are gone. The tree looks dead—but it's not.

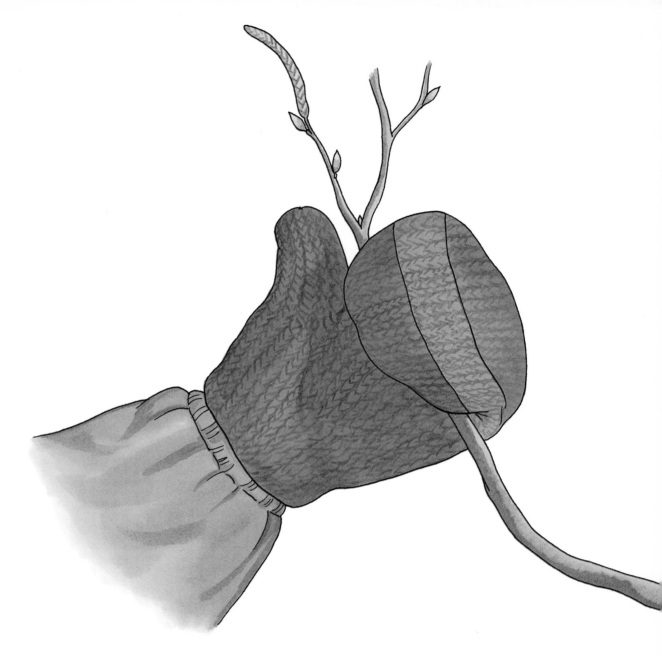

Look closely at a twig. Do you see the fat bud at the end? It will open and become a new, green leaf when spring comes.

What happened to the yellow dandelions
of summer? Look under the snow where
they used to be. The flowers are dead and
gone.

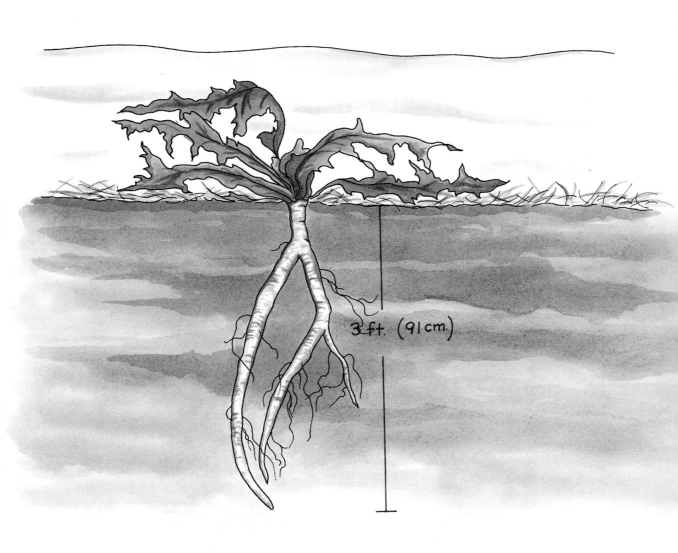

3 ft. (91 cm.)

But deep underground, the dandelions' roots stay alive. Next spring they will grow to make new yellow flowers.

Look at the pine trees. They stay green all winter long. Their pine cones have seeds hidden in them. What a treat for the hungry blue jays!

Though many birds fly to warmer places
for winter, some stay behind. Look down.
Do you see bird tracks in the snow?

Your boots make tracks in the snow too.
And look! There are more tracks.

Let's follow them to see where they lead.

The little tracks lead right to a tree. Shhh!
There's a snowshoe hare hidden under the
branches. She has grown a white fur coat
to match the snow. That makes her hard
to see.

The hare hides in the daytime from her enemy, the snowy owl. At night she hops about, looking for branches to nibble.

The beavers in the pond do not worry about finding food. They gathered food during the fall. Now they can stay safe and warm inside their lodge.

When the beavers get hungry, they just
swim under the ice to their food pile.

But where are the frogs and toads of the
pond? They have dug into the mud at the
bottom.

The frogs and toads won't move or eat
until spring comes.

All too soon the sun begins to set on a
winter afternoon. Look! Your long shadow
follows you home.

You can hardly wait to warm yourself in front of a toasty fire. Wintertime is the time for fires in the fireplace and hot cocoa in your cup.

Slowly the days of winter grow longer and warmer. Icicles melt quickly in the warm sunshine.

Then, one day, you find a little, yellow flower in bloom. What new season is about to begin?

MORE TO EXPLORE

Professor Facto says . . .
When it is winter on the top half of the
world, it is summer on the bottom half.
While children in North America are
playing in the snow, children in Australia
are playing at the beach! Ask an adult to
help you find where you live on a globe.
Do you live on the top half of the world or
the bottom half?

For the top half of the world, winter begins
around December 21. It ends around
March 21. Ask an adult to help you find
these dates on a calendar. Count the
number of Sundays from December 21 to
March 21 to find out how many weeks
long winter is. What holidays come in
winter? Is your birthday in winter?

Winter Shadows

If you went outside at noon on a summer day, you wouldn't have much of a shadow. That is because the sun would be high overhead.

Go outside at noon on a winter day and see where the sun is in the sky. Can you see your shadow? Is it long or short? Can you guess why?

Now play a game of shadow tag! To play, choose someone to be "it." "It" must try to step on someone else's shadow before the shadow gets away. If your shadow gets stepped on, you are "it"!

Plan Ahead!

Save a snowball in your freezer. Write the date on a piece of paper. Put it in a plastic bag with the snowball so you can remember when you made your snowball. On the first hot day of summer, reach into your freezer for a little bit of winter!

Making an "Ice Balloon"

What happens to water on the cold days of winter? What would happen to a water balloon? You can find out!

1. Fill a balloon with water and tie it shut. How does the water balloon feel?

2. Ask a friend to hold the water balloon by the knot at the end while you measure it. Take a long piece of string and wrap it around the fattest part of the balloon. Make a mark where the ends meet. Save the string for later.

3. Put the balloon outside on the snow. Leave it there overnight when the temperatures are below freezing.

4. When the water balloon feels like it has turned into an "ice balloon," bring it inside. Measure the balloon again with the string. Does it take more or less string to go around the ice balloon? Why is that? (Water stretches out as it freezes. It takes up more space. We say it **expands.**)

5. Now take off the balloon to see your "ice ball." How does it feel?

Bird Feeder Fun

Food is harder for birds to find in winter. You can help your feathered friends by making a bird feeder. Remember, if you begin feeding birds in early winter, you should continue until spring, for the birds will come to depend on you. Here are two kinds of bird feeders to make:

1. You will need a large pine cone, string, peanut butter, and bird seed. Tie string around the top of the pine cone and make a loop with the remaining string. Use a dull knife to fill the open areas of the pine cone with peanut butter. Roll the sticky pine cone in bird seed. The seeds will stick to the pine cone.

2. You will need a plastic milk jug, string, and bird seed. First make sure the plastic jug is cleaned out. Ask an adult to cut a large rectangle from both sides of the jug. Fill the bottom of the jug with bird seed. Tie string through the handle and around the neck of the bottle.

Now hang your bird feeders outside on a tree branch and wait for the birds to arrive!

INDEX